# The Shipwreck
## The Story of Paul's Rescue at Sea

We are grateful to the following team of authors for their contributions to *God Loves Me*, a Bible story program for young children. This Bible story, one of a series of fifty-two, was written by Patricia L. Nederveld, managing editor for CRC Publications. Suggestions for using this book were developed by Sherry Ten Clay, training coordinator for CRC Publications and freelance author from Albuquerque, New Mexico. Yvonne Van Ee, an early childhood educator, served as project consultant and wrote *God Loves Me*, the program guide that accompanies this series of Bible storybooks.

Nederveld has served as a consultant to Title I early childhood programs in Colorado. She has extensive experience as a writer, teacher, and consultant for federally funded preschool, kindergarten, and early childhood programs in Colorado, Texas, Michigan, Florida, Missouri, and Washington, using the *High/Scope* Education Research Foundation curriculum. In addition to writing the *Bible Footprints* church curriculum for four- and five-year-olds, Nederveld edited the revised *Threes* curriculum and the first edition of preschool through second grade materials for the *LiFE* curriculum, all published by CRC Publications.

Ten Clay taught preschool for ten years in public schools in California, Missouri, and North Carolina and served as a Title IV preschool teacher consultant in Kansas City. For over twenty-five years she has served as a church preschool leader and also as a MOPS (Mothers of Preschoolers) volunteer. Ten Clay is coauthor of the preschool-kindergarten materials of the *LiFE* curriculum published by CRC Publications.

Van Ee is a professor and early childhood program advisor in the Education Department at Calvin College, Grand Rapids, Michigan. She has served as curriculum author and consultant for Christian Schools International and wrote the original *Story Hour* organization manual and curriculum materials for fours and fives.

Photo on page 5: David J. Sams/Tony Stone Images; photo on page 20: Digital Stock.

**Library of Congress Cataloging-in-Publication Data**

Nederveld, Patricia L., 1944-
    The shipwreck: the story of Paul's rescue at sea/Patricia L. Nederveld.
      p. cm. — (God loves me; bk. 52)
    Summary: A rhyming retelling of the Bible story in which the Apostle Paul is rescued, along with more than two hundred others, when a storm wrecks their ship. Includes follow-up activities.
    ISBN 1-56212-321-1
    1. Paul, the Apostle, Saint—Journeys—Juvenile literature.
2. Shipwrecks in the Bible—Juvenile literature. [1. Paul, the Apostle, Saint. 2. Bible stories—N.T.] I. Title. II. Series: Nederveld, Patricia L., 1944- God loves me; bk. 52.
BS2506.5.N46 1998
226.6'09505—dc21

                                           98-15634
                                            CIP
                                            AC

10 9 8 7 6 5 4 3 2 1

# The Shipwreck
## The Story of Paul's Rescue at Sea

PATRICIA L. NEDERVELD

ILLUSTRATIONS BY PAUL STOUB

CRC Publications
Grand Rapids, Michigan

**T**his is a story from God's book, the Bible.

It's for  *say name(s) of your child(ren).*
It's for me too!

*Acts 27*

The sun shone bright, the sea looked calm
as the ship sailed away from the beach.

It was time for the trip to Italy—
a new place for Paul to preach!

But it wasn't long before something went wrong.
A fierce storm swept over the sea.

Waves rolled high, not a person stayed dry,
and the sailors were scared as can be!

Passengers too
were looking
quite blue—
too frightened to
eat just a bite!

There was only
one man who
remained
unafraid—
and he knelt down
to pray through
the night.

" The winds may blow, the waves may roll,
but my God made a promise to me.

No one will die—we all shall be safe.
Just trust in my God and you'll see!"

Then Paul took some bread and gave thanks to God. "Now eat this!" he said to his friends.

So they did—then they waited—and waited some more. Oh, when would this storm ever end?

But the waves smashed the ship and broke it apart. "Swim for shore!" came the captain's command!

So they jumped from the ship, they floated, they swam!
Yes, everyone headed toward land!

One, two, three, four—two hundred and more!
They all made it safely to shore.

Paul counted the crowd, then gave thanks to God.
"You saved us, dear God! Praise the Lord!"

I wonder if you know that Jesus loves you and keeps you safe too . . .

Dear Jesus, thank you for loving us so much. Help us to love you as much as Paul did. Amen.

# Suggestions for Follow-up

## Opening

Ahead of time, make enough copies of the large water drop (see Pattern Z, Patterns Section, *God Loves Me* program guide) so that each child has one or more. Attach a loop of masking tape to the back of each drop. Wear one on your shirt as you greet your little ones. Invite them to hang the drops in your room.

Gather your little ones together with a group hug. Thank God for keeping each one safe and for bringing you together.

## Learning Through Play

Learning through play is the best way! The following activity suggestions are meant to help you provide props and experiences that will invite the children to play their way into the Scripture story and its simple truth. Try to provide plenty of time for the children to choose their own activities and to play individually. Use group activities sparingly—little ones learn most comfortably with a minimum of structure.

1. Fill shallow dishpans or a baby bathtub with water. You may want to put a shower curtain liner under the tub. Encourage your little ones to move plastic boats across the water by blowing, pushing, or guiding them with a straw. Show them how to make waves, and watch the boats toss up and down. If you wish, provide other small objects and explore together which things float and which things sink. Imagine how afraid the sailors were that the ship would sink. But Paul knew Jesus would keep them safe!

2. Use one or more banana boxes taped together to form a boat large enough for your entire group. Or use masking tape or Velcro strips to mark a boat outline on the floor. Sit in the boat together to retell the story. As the storm builds, sway, then rock back and forth. Offer crackers to eat. Finally, encourage your little ones to swim to safety. Gather together to thank Jesus for keeping you safe.

3. Bring inflatable pool toys such as rafts or rings. Invite your little ones to ride the raft or wear the rings as they "swim" across the room. Wonder with them how it felt to ride through the storm and then swim for shore. Remember to thank God for keeping Paul safe.

4. Find a clear plastic jar with a lid (a peanut butter jar works well). As your little ones watch, fill the jar with water, then add a few drops of blue food coloring and a generous sprinkling of glitter. Glue the lid shut with tacky glue. Show the children how to shake the jar to make a glitter storm. Invite each one to take a turn. Talk about the storm that scared the sailors and how Paul prayed all night. Remind your little ones that Jesus kept Paul safe, and he will keep them safe too.

5. Provide sheets of construction paper, blue tempera paint, and straws. Place a few drops of paint on the paper, and show your children how to blow the paint with the straw. (Younger children may need help mastering this trick.) Talk about the rolling waves and the stormy sea—but God saved Paul!

6. Help your little ones celebrate God's care for them with this action rhyme:

> *God keeps me safe each day.* (clap, clap)
> *God keeps me safe each day.* (clap, clap)
> *I belong to God. Hurray!* (clap, clap)
> *I know God keeps me safe each day.* (clap, clap)

—© 1992, CRC Publications

Children will also enjoy stomping their feet or shaking maracas instead of clapping. If you wish, sing the rhyme (Songs Section, *God Loves Me* program guide).

## Closing

Invite each child to take a water drop from the walls and bring it to your group circle. Show them how to stick the drop to their shirts. Then move around the outside of the circle, and touch each child gently as you thank God for keeping each one safe. Give each of your little ones a goodbye hug as they leave.

## At Home

Safety is an important issue for parents and a topic that provides many opportunities to teach your little one about God's care. Together praise God for things and people that keep your child safe: seat belts, car seats, outlet covers, trusted neighbors, and caregivers. Invite your little one to join you at mealtime and bedtime to thank God for caring for your family throughout the day.

## Old Testament Stories

**Blue and Green and Purple Too!** *The Story of God's Colorful World*

**It's a Noisy Place!** *The Story of the First Creatures*

**Adam and Eve** *The Story of the First Man and Woman*

**Take Good Care of My World!** *The Story of Adam and Eve in the Garden*

**A Very Sad Day** *The Story of Adam and Eve's Disobedience*

**A Rainy, Rainy Day** *The Story of Noah*

**Count the Stars!** *The Story of God's Promise to Abraham and Sarah*

**A Girl Named Rebekah** *The Story of God's Answer to Abraham*

**Two Coats for Joseph** *The Story of Young Joseph*

**Plenty to Eat** *The Story of Joseph and His Brothers*

**Safe in a Basket** *The Story of Baby Moses*

**I'll Do It!** *The Story of Moses and the Burning Bush*

**Safe at Last!** *The Story of Moses and the Red Sea*

**What Is It?** *The Story of Manna in the Desert*

**A Tall Wall** *The Story of Jericho*

**A Baby for Hannah** *The Story of an Answered Prayer*

**Samuel! Samuel!** *The Story of God's Call to Samuel*

**Lions and Bears!** *The Story of David the Shepherd Boy*

**David and the Giant** *The Story of David and Goliath*

**A Little Jar of Oil** *The Story of Elisha and the Widow*

**One, Two, Three, Four, Five, Six, Seven!** *The Story of Elisha and Naaman*

**A Big Fish Story** *The Story of Jonah*

**Lions, Lions!** *The Story of Daniel*

## New Testament Stories

**Jesus Is Born!** *The Story of Christmas*

**Good News!** *The Story of the Shepherds*

**An Amazing Star!** *The Story of the Wise Men*

**Waiting, Waiting, Waiting!** *The Story of Simeon and Anna*

**Who Is This Child?** *The Story of Jesus in the Temple*

**Follow Me!** *The Story of Jesus and His Twelve Helpers*

**The Greatest Gift** *The Story of Jesus and the Woman at the Well*

**A Father's Wish** *The Story of Jesus and a Little Boy*

**Just Believe!** *The Story of Jesus and a Little Girl*

**Get Up and Walk!** *The Story of Jesus and a Man Who Couldn't Walk*

**A Little Lunch** *The Story of Jesus and a Hungry Crowd*

**A Scary Storm** *The Story of Jesus and a Stormy Sea*

**Thank You, Jesus!** *The Story of Jesus and One Thankful Man*

**A Wonderful Sight!** *The Story of Jesus and a Man Who Couldn't See*

**A Better Thing to Do** *The Story of Jesus and Mary and Martha*

**A Lost Lamb** *The Story of the Good Shepherd*

**Come to Me!** *The Story of Jesus and the Children*

**Have a Great Day!** *The Story of Jesus and Zacchaeus*

**I Love You, Jesus!** *The Story of Mary's Gift to Jesus*

**Hosanna!** *The Story of Palm Sunday*

**The Best Day Ever!** *The Story of Easter*

**Goodbye—for Now** *The Story of Jesus' Return to Heaven*

**A Prayer for Peter** *The Story of Peter in Prison*

**Sad Day, Happy Day!** *The Story of Peter and Dorcas*

**A New Friend** *The Story of Paul's Conversion*

**Over the Wall** *The Story of Paul's Escape in a Basket*

**A Song in the Night** *The Story of Paul and Silas in Prison*

**A Ride in the Night** *The Story of Paul's Escape on Horseback*

**The Shipwreck** *The Story of Paul's Rescue at Sea*

## Holiday Stories

Selected stories from the New Testament to help you celebrate the Christian year

**Jesus Is Born!** *The Story of Christmas*

**Good News!** *The Story of the Shepherds*

**An Amazing Star!** *The Story of the Wise Men*

**Hosanna!** *The Story of Palm Sunday*

**The Best Day Ever!** *The Story of Easter*

**Goodbye—for Now** *The Story of Jesus' Return to Heaven*

These fifty-two books are the heart of *God Loves Me,* a Bible story program designed for young children. Individual books (or the entire set) and the accompanying program guide *God Loves Me* are available from CRC Publications (1-800-333-8300).